LINES

Ian Ritchie **LINES**

ROYAL ACADEMY OF ARTS

Editor
Tom Neville

Designer
Claudia Schenk

Printed by Henry Ling Limited

Cover image: Fluy House

British Library Cataloguing-in-Publication Data
A catalogue record of this book is available from the
British Library

ISBN 978-1-905711-81-9

Distributed outside the United States and Canada by
Thames & Hudson Ltd, London
Distributed in the United States and Canada by
Harry N. Abrams, Inc., New York

CONTENTS

A QUARTET FOR IAN

by Roger McGough

Aphorisms sown.
Green shoots of poems appear.
Plans laid, lines are drawn.

Space sculptor standing
outside the box, thinking in.
A dream taking shape.

*   *   *

Outside of dream space
sculptor shoots green aphorisms.
Haiku taking shape.

Taking, standing the.
Plans sown are laid in a box.
Lines appear poems.

May 2010

We will finesse
the fineness
of emptiness.

Still in winter.

Balanced plane
of *levitas*
and *gravitas*.

Music from silence.

'John Cage's writings have implanted (at least) two important
ideas: music grows out of silence and paradoxically, there is no
silence, since the sounds of the world are invasive.'
    David Toop, Sonic Boom, *Hayward Gallery, 2000, an*
    exhibition designed by Ian Ritchie Architects

The difference between architecture and sculpture is that the former has functioning toilets

EARLY THOUGHTS FOR BERMONDSEY STATION

We can measure the temperature of light,
but can we feel the colour of the wind?
The sensuality of underground public space
must bring the outside climate down.

The flow of the Thames is in the soil.
It marks the direction of travel
and mirrors the daily passage of the sun
which ought to resonate in our design.

In a world which is hurry hurry,
and rougher rougher, can a calmer calmer,
slower slower place be allowed
as part of London's Underground?

We must touch light, touch the soil.
We must feel the temperature,
we must smell the wind
and paint colours in our mind.

A framed emptiness
brings down the sky
to meet the earth.
Diaphanous shell
stretched taut over
squared silhouettes
of thin round metal.

Light chases darkness.
Shadows are holes
in light. Colours flow
throughout the space.
Sunlight and cloud,
the shadows come and go.

Light is our umbrella against the sky

ALBA DI MILANO (DAWN OF MILAN)

Alba is an arc, so subtle it is almost
    imperceptible.
The desire to reach the heavens asks man to
    overcome the arc,
this escaping arc that simply manifests gravity,
whether through the solid arrow from a bow,
or curving water falling from a spout,
or a luminous November rocket fading away,
has held us entranced for centuries.
Man eventually made it, but now we ask for
    what purpose.
Humankind's lifeboat may exist one day,
and find new water upon which to float and
    drink
thanks to the diminished arc,
but the future may deem that we simply
    changed a letter.
Arc for ark, and another myth for man.

Light is <u>the</u> material of architecture

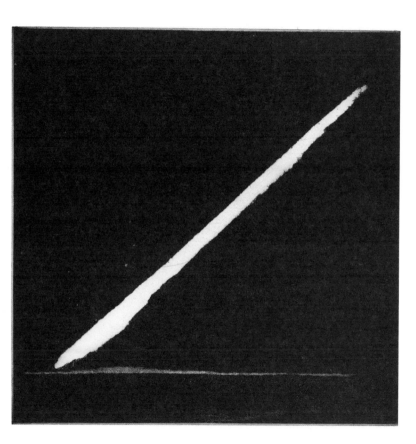

NATURE'S CURVE

Bitumen roads and steel rails
slide across the countryside
marking the flow of contours,
just as the viaduct's comb
measures its topography.

Of all our infrastructures,
power lines ignore Earth's curves,
forming catenary lines
without much affinity.

Hanging these transmission wires,
the skeletal Goliaths stride
miles across rolling hills,
grey imperious warriors.

We'll design for our own age,
with a new aesthetic form
responding to the landscape,
far more in tune with nature.

Progress is no longer the idea that just because we can means we should

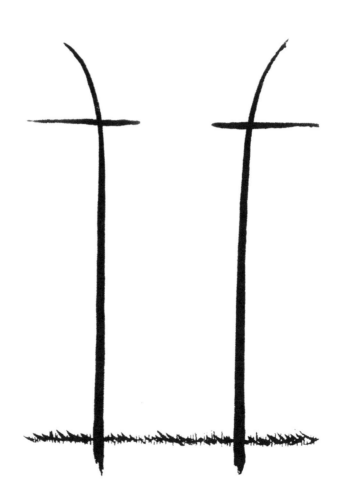

A fragment of a greenhouse
within a landscape of fragments
from imagined continents.

Where the sun is big
and the wind is yellow.

Where the mass of the Earth
meets the lightness of the air.

Where walls are walls,
not covered up,
the same inside as outside
and we can act within and without.

Where our accumulated culture
cannot cover the walls
and cracks in the walls are real
and do not worry us.

Where the roof is a lake
but opaque to water and wind,
a virtual surface for the heavens,
where water is both real and imaginary.
Where the sun is big
and imagination is free.

Where rough does not touch smooth,
where the earth does not touch the sky.
Only wavelengths change
and we get hot.

Where the sun is big.

Our earth is simply the natural greenhouse of our solar-system home

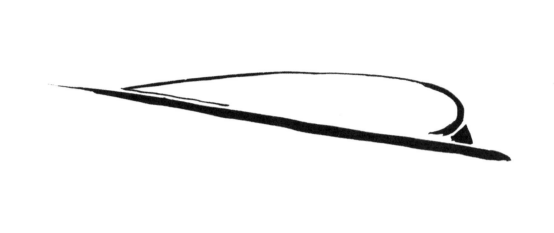

A monument inspired by the light
of Ireland's ever-changing skies,
ever present by day and by night.

Tall, elegant, conical structure
symbolising growth, search, release,
thrust, optimism in Ireland's future.

Granite anchored underneath the street,
sliding past a bronze spiral base
a shell of peened silver stainless steel.

Urban line and point upon the site
softly reflecting sunlit clouds
while swaying in the wind, a night-light.

Light is the opium of the architect and shadow its form

UNDERGROUND WINDS

Builders' grilles and louvres
somehow fail to reflect
the motion of air
and its non-linear qualities
of turbulence and pressure.

I would like to develop
an architecture in landscapes
(where leaves show us the motions of wind)
that allow the man-made winds
below the land to kiss free air.

I am convinced that beauty is in large measure non-linear

FRESH STONE

Risk floating, flotsam flesh
every time you put the kettle on,
for someone may, yes,
drown in Bangladesh.

Wasted steam, last breath –
water is a battleground
between energy
and uncontrolled death.

'Men's evil manners live in brass;
their virtues we write in water.'
Oh Keats, tombed Romantic pen,
what will come to pass?

Carbon filters for Africa,
carbon dioxide for all of us.
Is ice Earth's fresh stone?
Glacier, rain, clean our air.

I am motivated by ideas because they have values – physical, intellectual, social and economic

PIN-STRIPED BUSINESSMEN

Pin-striped businessmen
capture the spirit of our time:
hurry hurry hurry to
money money money to
plane plane plane to
where how when
rush rush males
leaving vapour trails
in an English country garden
that is more a sea of Sierras.
We'll find an elegant solution
by maximising the areas,
and while the rules may be written
innovation is not forbidden.
'And by the way, keep inside the budget
and give us the key on time.'

A little repetition refines, excessive repetition stalls the mind

PLANES OF GUERNICA

Grey, black, white planes of Guernica,
layers of history before me,
the painting tells me to 'capture' her
and let Reina Sofia's building go free.

Reina Sofia's new museum of modern art
begins with Guernica – it's the key,
and I am charged with designing the part
that creates its new identity.

The prison bars need spreading apart
and by redefining them I can see
captured freedom, and Guernica's art
as an expression of modernity.

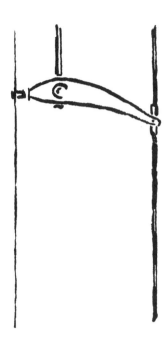

CATENARY LANDSCAPE

Aircraft appear on water
in a liquid landscape where
the sun rises above a basin
and sets behind a rising city.
Two competitive rowers
dream a fantastic building.
Others decline the work,
offering us a chance to plan
how two buildings can be one
where docks tighten into a throat
on a tight triangle of land.
By impressing new walls upon old walls
made of destructed empire warehouses,
emerging powerful forms
can shape the dockside again,
not with thin corrugated sheet
but with caged undulating minerals.

Every collaboration is a chance to grow

DRIFTWOOD

A city of waves
crushes an armada
at sea.
Stranded driftwood
flotsam history,
unknown stories
in each piece.
Like plays
without words,
these memories
are silent,
pregnant with
potential they sit
on the rocks.
Seagulls poised
on bowsprits,
reflected colours
in permanent
movement
on waves
that bring back
stories.

Been here before,
singing and dancing, inside,
an audience suspended
in a stone-wrapped steel shell.

A park within which to grow
space and lines,
first traced upon the ground
then folded into forms.

The ground and the sky
belong to each other.
Pencils springing
between earth and cloud.

Drawing people together.

The only certainty about certainty is its uncertainty

Green scrubs,
grey waste
within a city,
to make whitecity.

Railways everywhere,
outside, inside and underneath,
and an absurd motorway
disturb a site in which lie dead
exhibition walkways.
And are these to be buried
with a few thousand cars
beneath air-conditioned malls?

Or, a new citadel for London
with a large walled garden
and market square,
maybe a twenty-first-century city souk
where we feel wind, sun and rain?

Is there an imaginary commercial landscape
of butterflies and honey,
of greenbelt and Gucci belt,
of bamboos and balloons?

Architecture has two distinct phases: the mental dream and the nightmare of negotiating reality

This Crossrail station will lie beneath the water,
a symbolic idea that allows water to stay
dominant and to comfort our eyes in this urban
    scene.

There is so much human energy visible
that had exploited water and motion
to build an empire of trade with the world.

This energy is now invisible,
buried beneath glass and steel towers
of another empire that trades electrons.

Regret, yes, for a lost opportunity to
refloat London's new financial market on
waterways so generous and welcoming.

A new fluid city, gifted by labour's history,
and allowed to gather fluidity
as the wind waves the grasses.

Strange how the visible – water, so beautiful,
so important now and in the future –
is made less and less visible as the invisible
economy takes over.

A canopy – red or golden – will float in the air
above the water to prevent heaven's water
wetting the travelling man and his electron pad.

The book everyone bought
but few ever read.

Cosmos of Big Bang,
black holes,
singularity,
an architecture
inside space and time
of great expansion,
of stars exploding
within brilliant minds.

Before Hawking's time
Anaximander
first thought of deep space;
Pythagoras's spheres,
Aristotle's proof
of Earth's sphericity,
Aristarchus's and
Copernicus's sun-
centred universe,
Hipparchus's brightness
scale of the stars
and the Earth's wobble,

Ptolemy's theory,
Omar Khayyam's year
and Galileo's
incarceration,
Kepler's ellipses
Newtonian physics,
and Albert Einstein's
Relativity –
mass and energy
determine spacetime
geometry
and the curvatures
of spacetime express
themselves in forces –
gravitational.

Such breathtaking thoughts
at the project's heart,
imagination
to engage and thrill.

As we search for freedom
another seeks orchids.
As we learn to build
another dreams of a house.

A parent bird, an eagle
and her young offspring,
lead thoughts of redefining
home as a suitcase with wings.

A bird carrying a suitcase,
so free, yet so tied to history.
Is there a house in liberty
that has an open suitcase?

EAGLE ROCK

Nous émergeons lentement d'un
environnement lourd,
nous évoluons vers un environnement léger.
L'environnement lourd –
la centralisation politique,
l'aliénation personnelle,
les constructions anonymes,
et l'architecture anti-climatique
ont posé les jalons d'une évolution
vers un environnement léger
où les individus et les sociétés pourront
    exprimer
une réponse sensuelle à la vie…
faire vivre la démocratie.

To live
beneath a well-insulated umbrella.
To live
from space to space with sun and
to sense the rhythm of the seasons.

Light moves and changes space

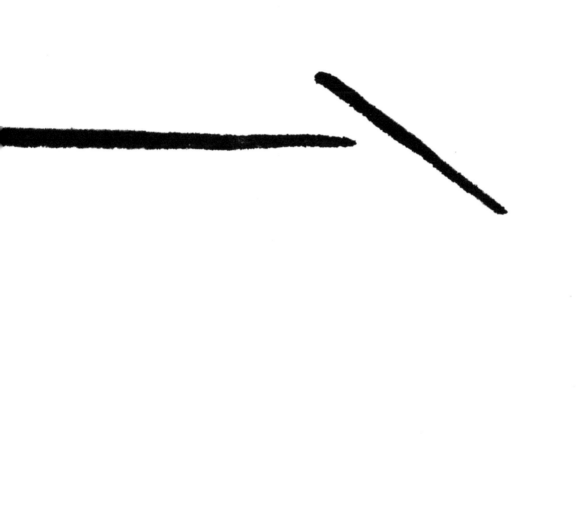

If it's rusty,
and it's red,
recyclable and temporary
then the beginning will begin.
And tomorrow
our translated scheme
welcomes more
summer dreams
than we can imagine.
Stand firm, deliver, perform and
thé th_rusty space will live.

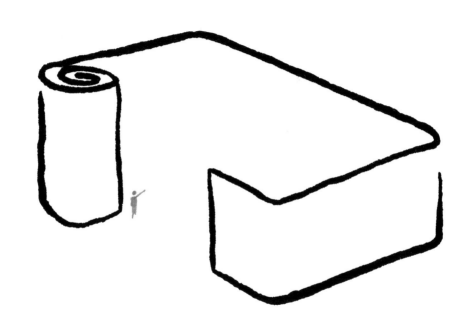

A ring of beauty,
silent, brilliant,
motionless
and floating.

Woven titanium
reflecting ring,
electronic
hieroglyphs.

A landscape without,
painting within,
part of me
and others.

A place where the dreams
of so many
appear still
and dreaming.

Communications,
magnetic energy
hovers this
singing ring.

Transcribed from notes as a result of the Japanese client moving the
site from the sea in Osaka Bay to the top of Awaji Island.

Smart taxi driver,
nice ride.
Happy going
around and around
Rocket Junction pub,
Queens Drive,
and the M62.

Imagining and thinking,
why do I like this city of
the Reds, the Kop, the music,
home of my alma mater?
Red is covering the city,
and my memories
of Red nights in Europe,
and blues nights.

A sculpted arc will go nowhere,
and mean nothing.
This is no site for empty gestures
but one for people on a bridge
to wave at the stream
of multicoloured metal fish –
Liverpudlians
welcoming people.

Reintroduced to antiquity
alongside feathers and fur,
kites and coins,
prints and spaces unseen
for decades.

A museum of the world
in a world inhabited by a dreamer,
wanting for its future
a role, a perspective,
something publicly tangible.

An estate of a million square feet,
plus a few bits and pieces
scattered north and west
about London
filled with ten million worlds.

A dream begins with an experience,
a visit, a new dimension,
a new way of seeing the same objects;
excited, as a family, the www,
a world exploding myths.

A journey that discovers
at every turn beauty, knowledge,
craft and language,
a chance to twist centuries past
into centuries forward.

Objects first, space everywhere,
husbandry, caring, learning;
disseminating understanding,
sharing space, spaces,
experiment, enlighten.

A centre without meaning,
a place of contemplation
with nothing to contemplate. How come?
Give me a look-out
to announce that we can see beyond ourselves.

A place to shout, to sound a bell,
a minaret, a campanile to balance
the empty dome.
Brave new museum,
what a wonder you can become.

We have to distinguish not only between fact and fiction but also between communication and discourse

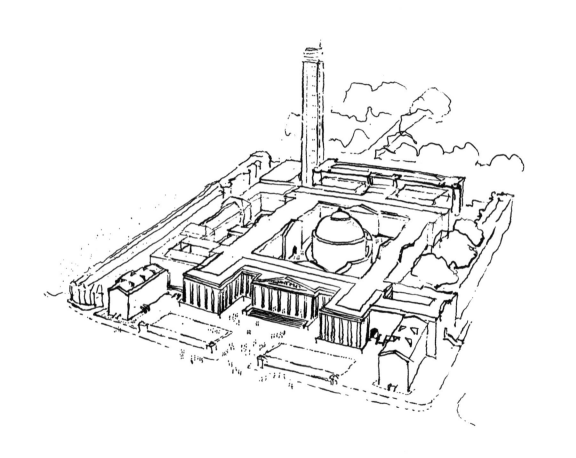

More than architectural
is a carbon-negative scheme.
Beyond carbon neutral.

How to achieve such a scheme?
Design for life, to house for life
without being extreme.

Orientate, shade for summer,
make use of the laws of physics,
insulate for winter.

Engage the wind energy,
DC to AC to DC,
not waste a guarantee.

And if you don't get a bill
but a payment every quarter
it's a marketing thrill.

A touch of borehole cooling
and some solar vacuum tubes
to reduce the fuelling.

Compost the vegetable waste,
rainwater to be collected,
recycle to replace.

And finally, if we build
with higher flood levels in mind,
a future is fulfilled.

We're not running out of energy but out of atmosphere

They want to build again,
having built so badly
on land so visually precious.

There is no image
of any architecture that deserves
more prominence than the rocks.

To hide is not to be weak,
but to be intelligent
faced with such beauty.

A horizontal streak of red stone
among the columnar basalt.
Perhaps a clue?

A natural surprise,
locked in the land
between blue sky, grass and sea.

Man comes to trample
upon a giant's step.
Look back, look down, think.

Did I see any architecture
other than nature's own?
No.

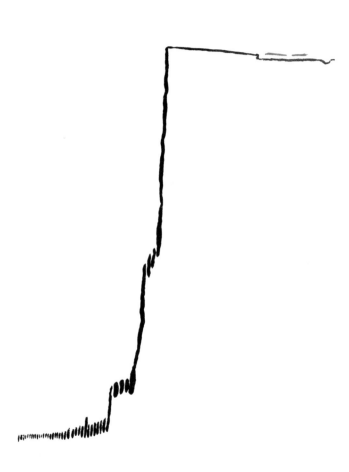

A client I do not understand,
but whose father is a friend.
A client with few funds
and a site on a flood plain
will require a very particular strategy.

Moholy-Nagy once made coloured tiles
by phoning his ceramicist.
Perhaps, fifty years on,
With phone and fax
a building made in the south
can be assembled in the north.

I'll need to work with someone I can trust.
Ah, Monsieur Viry, a man of steel
with energy and humour.
A client I do not have to meet
can then have his building.

What is the currency of communication that enables collaboration?

The suspended
white ceiling overhead
has far too many lamps
and consumes too much power.

We need task light
efficient and bright
running only ten watts,
giving fifteen hundred lux.

Sequel: when it comes to a name

He said 'goodnight'
and switched off the light,
the eco-minded spring
from *The Magic Roundabout*,
Zebedee ('time for bed').

Like an object moving through water, light cuts through shadows only to leave shadows in its wake

TIP-TOE TABLE

On tip-toe,
three feet apart
and two toes
resting on the earth.

A white horizon floats,
reflecting life, about
which we question
with our resting hands.

Silver frame
four feet across,
one rounded ring
supporting life.

TURVILLE SUN

Cosmic capture
sunbeams measure
the turning world,
the running sand
where beasts roam
and silver logs
appear fallen
among sheep,
and blossom
perfumes time
in a timeless
garden,
our Earth
cycles its magic
as we count the hours.
Circle, and marker
pointing to the sky
and an occasional blue disc.
And the sky
rests on the green grass.

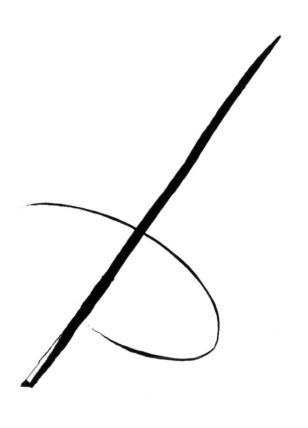

A special step with upward stride
across mountain or stream,
a movement sublime.

No fallen tree or gymnast
to carry me across this river,
only a floating arc of light.

Shallow river, deep texts
reflecting history flowing beneath
a slender arch, and time is still.

Architecture is synthesis not separation – the synthesis of ideas, of people,
of materials and ultimately the synthesis of the manmade with nature

The ebb and flow of life:
we seem to move in circles,
sometimes incomplete.

In silent thought,
an unexpected view
becomes panoramic.

Lost in dreams,
an invisible bird sings
for me as the mist lifts.

Sunrise, sunset, moon
beyond a curved branch;
a leaf falls, nearby.

Sinuous form of life
unfolding within the mind
across a landscape.

Reclining, twice placed
upon the grass together,
or sometimes alone.

Thoughts construct a seat
at a specific place
under a white moon.

Rolled silvery steel,
hardwood touching softness,
caressing the light.

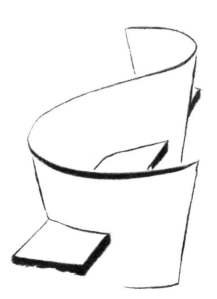

Slip, tide, river
cross me, slowly,
watch the light
dance upon me.

Slide, stroll, river
cross me, happily,
let the air
caress my cheeks.

Time to ponder
solid sliding arc,
red as sun
setting.

The power of aesthetics is measured in the mind, not in the bank balance or
electricity meter. The lack of it is like drip water torture, it numbs the mind

Dubai is a strange new city
of old culture and leisure
in search of identity.

Sea life, water and energy
drive this hot environment.
But what of its memory?

Once famous for pearls and gold,
all the pearls have been farmed,
and now oil and gas are sold.

A new monument, a sphere,
seventeen metres across,
of cool glass, lustrous and sheer.

Doubly curved opalescent skin,
translucent, iridescent,
floating pearl, museum within.

No triangulation line,
no longitude, latitude,
a new pattern to design.

A pentagon and a square –
Keith Laws, Ensor Holiday
stitch them with geometric flair.

The arabesque-patterned surface
glass panels and rod structure
enclose a luminous space.

Along the Deira to the Creek
it becomes a new symbol
of Dubai's culture, unique.

The values we admire in public buildings are difficult to value

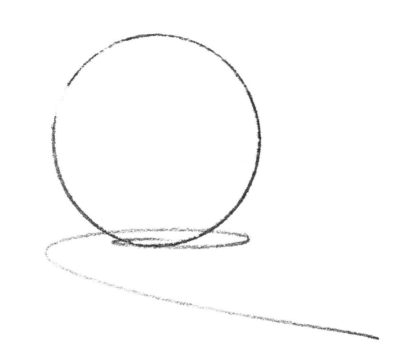

Fifteenth-century castle squared solid against the bay,
soldiers, westerly winds and storm tides, cross-section
sufficient to have given this French connection –
the ex-Norman Clanricardes, the whole of Galway.

The Clanricardes's great fortune will have ebbed and
    flowed.
Lady Leslie, cousin of Churchill, managed to bring
the castle, after the second world war, to the king.
Their nature and arts create a welcome abode.

The light, falcon and printer, rolling hair, Irish
    strength here
in this unique seascape, white-water-edged green-
    grey
rough rock shoreline, orange sun, a stunning bay,
and this massive stone keep, silhouette, black, austere.

So many Irish have been lost from Galway Bay
to the sea and to America, and no man here
matters more than any other, nor woman, nor tear.
This is a world where strength is vital every day.

Here, the crowded earth is far away, the loneliness
of being human to the fore, to protect what's left
of the wild, an environment being raped, theft
of a coast by people who couldn't care less.

Friendship locks in like the weather for the weekend.
Fire, song, wine, wit, others drop by, vitality
all touched by a shared art, culture, a reality
that there's a desire to live, protect and defend.

Oranmore Lands for a primary school in a far field,
the castle's near field is safe, its furthest craves
an approach that could build a curtain wall that
    braves
the winds, conceals the buildings, an ultimate shield.

I see this curtain as an incline of stone groynes
that would be perceived as one from across the bay,
squared castle in the foreground catching the spray.
No sign of any houses, a new landscape joins
the Oranmore Lands with the shore at Galway Bay.

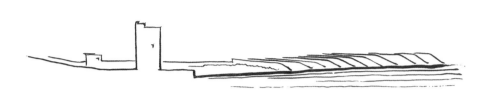

UNDERGROUND LIMPET

We stand on the curving black beach,
we wait, eyeing the line for a sign
of the arriving train, a spark, a screech
of metal upon metal, train on time.

The viaduct a hundred and fifty years ago
carried top hats and more cloth caps
into a town of smoking stacks; though
now mostly gone, the stains still show.

Our design will be a linear limpet,
clamped into the leaking brick vaults,
a challenge that will be a real sweat,
a project route forward as clear as fog.

Hugging the sides, the limpet passes beneath
and then leaps across the Central Line
to become the new concourse in a sheath
of silver steel with a golden lining.

We're responsible and cannot afford an error,
to imagine, with live lines above and below,
in an age of default positions and terror,
the spaces being built by day and by night.

We're going to need to make our own luck
to realise a delightful architecture
when everyone wants to pass the buck
From LUL to TfL, it'll come down to us.

How could we, the fans, allow our club,
to be hijacked by Americans?
Now it's time to go down to the pub,
us, the innocent, enraged fans!

We talked about it down in West Derby,
in Anfield, and up Brownlow Hill.
Fans all over the world are angry,
from Iceland to Spain, even in Brazil.

Koppite when we beat Honved two–nil,
the 'pool forty-odd year ago
just heaving with deep-down pride, just brill'.
How'll the new owners ever know?

We could have had Moores' shares in our hands,
if only he'd given us a chance.
But no, someone said, yeah, Americans,
who've led the board a merry dance.

Dear Hicks, Gillett and Mr Parry,
we've come up with this new design,
less cost, and far less debt to carry
for us supporters for our shrine.

For less than three hundred million pounds,
striking, iconic, for us and our team,
it'll seat seventy-odd-thousand fans –
a great Kop, great team, a great dream.

One hundred and fifty million pounds
that's become half a billion quid!
So down the pub lads for another round,
to work out how to make a bid.

Great architecture should connect technology to emotion, and space to the soul

The small family apartment has been
the 'sole normal housing unit' of the twentieth
    century.
Its morphological evolution can be seen
as social messages of salvation and hygiene
from prisons, barracks, workers' lodgings,
and hospital dormitories.

The houses in our cities consist
of three recognised alternatives:
terraced house, urban cottage (bliss),
and the apartment block. Let's reminisce.
Early twentieth-century reformers focused
on family values, equality and hygiene.

These three typologies are still endemic
as we move towards the twenty-first century.
We need to respond, without being too
    academic,
to changing needs – flexibility is the polemic.
The nature of housing units is the imperative;
flexibility reflects intelligent use of all resources.

A radical reappraisal of the way we design
and construct housing and how we fund it
is the key to delivering the quantum we pine
    for.
But in the end, is not the bottom line
the deep-rooted prejudice and preconceptions
of what a house, an apartment looks like –
    inside and outside?

Living in a capital museum-rich city centre
is moving towards the choice of the affluent.
Here pride of place is shared with those who
    enter
as tourist or down-and-out or those wanting
    adventure.
By contrast, living in the 'periphery' has little
    pride-of-place,
ecological density, mixture, diversity or
    flexibility.

We must raise the question of 'time'.
The time we spend living here or there,
living space versus living time.

Design and sculpt space using nature's own light pen

If living rather than subsistence time
is increasing, what amount will be spent
in the living space of the home or city?

At the moment we have few measures.
Individuals may be passing more and more
time in global virtuality, seeking pleasures.
The antithesis – local reality, family treasures –
requires new thinking about the balance
between a virtual and a physical haven
against the fast, rough, tough world we're all in.

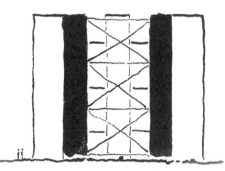

With less than four months to find a new place,
see a building that needs an extension,
make a planning submission straight away,
sort the bank without delay.

When extending an existing building
the usual architectural move
is to allow light to be the best glue
between the old and the new.

Do we take down the ceiling, go for space?
How wide to cut the light beam through the
    roof?
Should we also make one through the floor?
And we'll need a new front door!

Silver-white furniture, floor will be blue,
walls, chimneys inevitably white.
Tea point or kitchen, storage or workshop?
Plans, build, there's no time to stop!

Later, when time is available,
we revisit the extension design.
Change glass areas, a detail, too much glare,
the work's all done, and now we're there.

As the banks crashed
the fishing began.
We watched fish fly,
new-born lambs jump
and architects worry
about the next job.

Are architects magicians?
Bankers manipulated
and spirited away
immense substance,
but, above all,
loyalty and trust.

What do magicians do?
The science of magic?
As neuroscientists
research the mind
magicians play with it.
How?
Do they misdirect us?
Divert our attention?
Blind us temporarily?

Do they fill in the gaps?
Fill in the margins between
the frames of a film?
We imagine, we fill in.

And then there is memory.
Under which cup is the ball?
What card did I pick?
Ah, the magician has secrets!
The illusion of free will.
And, as now with the bankers,
do we mistrust the magician?

Architects are not magicians.
They are dreamers.
My architecture starts
in the spaces I create in my mind.
Space is in here and out there, it is a continuum
between inside and outside, mental and
    physical.
Now I am designing with the mind in mind.
Dreams? I try to build mine
avoiding the nightmares.

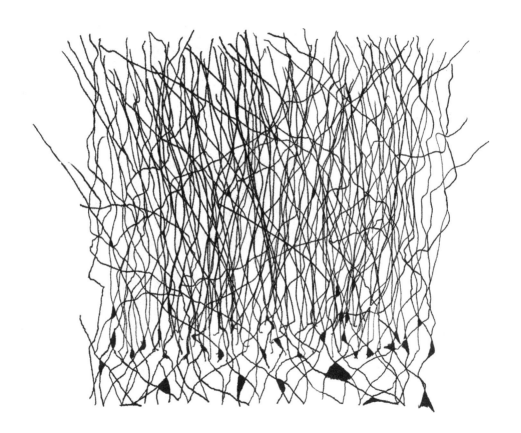

A billion-pound project
upon the stables' roof,
and what will they expect –
financiers and Chelsfield
and London Underground –
safety, an increased yield?
White City sitting pretty
and the stables working
architecturally.

Farming to Olympics,
football to festivals,
architectural tricks?
New Central Line siding,
sixteen trains overnight.
A new form of stabling?
Tunnels riddle the site,
a hidden cathedral
to overcome the blight.

One fundamental reading of the history of architecture is the story of the way light enters buildings

Another European competition
but one imbued with real hope.
an industrial ethos, even aesthetic,
reminiscent of the Courtyard in Stratford.
Was our RSC theatre their inspiration?

Or is this the cynical face of Europe,
the town that has its favourite son and
we merely players making up numbers
to help secure the Euros
with which the town can build?

Who knows? The project appeals:
the language and drama of theatre
have inbuilt passion, the unexpected,
the magic of thought, of word, of jest.
Yes. Fold the industrial curtain and reveal!

Is wood stuck on architecture simply the acceptable face of Western sustainable architecture?

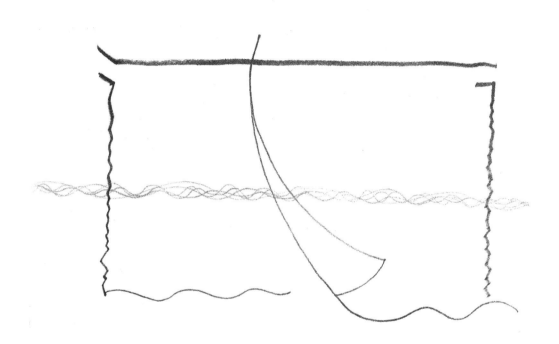

Into the low plain of Europe
where leafless howls of winter
sing to the endless grey sky
drives the BMW enterprise
to replenish Europe's grey streams
with more blue-white metal fish.

In gold waving fields of summer
under an azure sky,
thinking of more banal sheds
cannot change the key architect's brief:
to complete, simply, the office space
between three gigantic sheds.

Metal airborne conveyor belts
are required – they'll give drama
to spaces made for humans,
beyond which the world is robotic,
of sparking armed assembly lines
inside three gigantic sheds.

How could we change these monoliths
that greyscape the city fringe?
Is there a typology
that, once created, would dance
with waving fields of summer
and enchant us in winter?

Same shape, same cladding, a sameness
of bland boxes that contain
the making and the storage
of man's production and consumption.
The meeting space is the focus
but the walls are what matters.

If we do not design for all the senses, then we are surely designing for part-robots

They're still celebrating the opaque
wall coming down.
We, a handful of architectural players,
recognise these walls,
rebuilt all over Berlin,
regular stone-clothed buildings
with only a little glass.

What should a new British embassy reflect?
An open democracy, warmth, a welcome.
And what of sovereignty?
Is it as virginity,
something you have or have not?
There is no in-between, except
perhaps when you are the Foreign Office.

Is neighbourliness everything and nothing?
Don't stand out, meld the walls.
Don't think too deeply,
be discrete, certainly not Latin,
be not bold, follow Berlin's fashion
through diplomatic eyes.
Will stone conceal a perfidious Albion?

The art of architectural diplomacy is to engage through illusion to reach your conclusion

STONE SKIPPING

A stone bounced across the water,
imagining the same with tourist coins.
From the rich south bank of Greenwich
flows the museum's investment to the north.

The stone, the coin, the earth responds
accepting, holding and folding, becomes
the harbour of old and new boats
discreetly submerged, a new boat museum.

Our current notion of freedom is a handicap to progress.
Connexity, the essence of interdependence, is a way forward

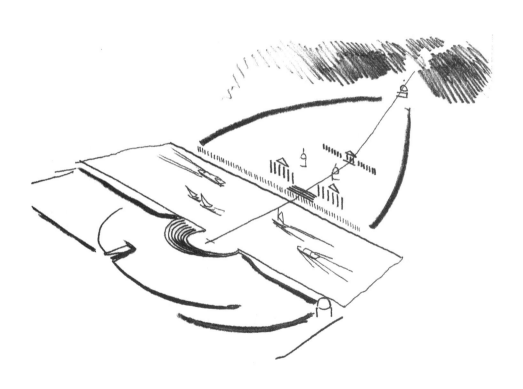

On Anglesey,
a pre-Roman Celtic haven,
stone burial chambers, standing stones,
and hill forts on the edge
of the Roman Empire.
And Tacitus talked of frightful Druids.
A landing stage for Dublin kings
to war with the Welsh.
A target for the Vikings
but resisted by the Christians
of St Cybi at Holyhead.
Home of Owain Tudor who
gave us Henry VIII and Elizabeth I.
Unearthed copper,
a growing port,
closest to Ireland,
and now for the tourists,
Telford's suspension bridge
across the Menai Straits
eased their travels.

Then the railway arrived
with Stephenson's Britannia Bridge.
Transport-engineering masters.
The copper hill emptied
but zinc, lead, gold and silver
still lie beneath those standing stones
as PlayStation games
transfix a young generation.
Finally in Holyhead water,
on Anglesey, three very tall
and unmissable
thin granite menhirs,
one round, one square and one cruciform,
stand on a triangular dolphin
twisting and piercing the sky,
as laden ferries come and go.

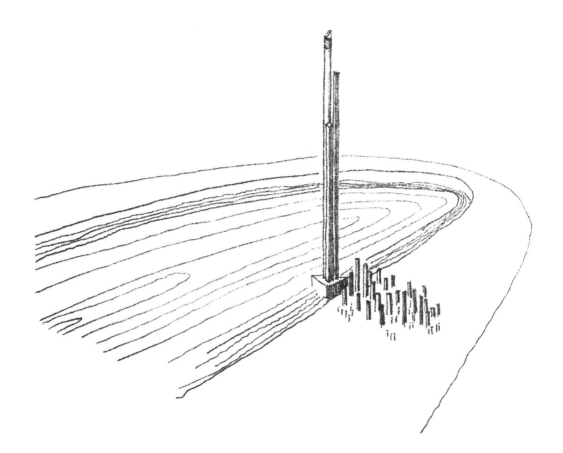

A people of persons,
despite the ebb and flow of their diasporas.
With feet on the ground,
a shadow cast is home.
Under the sun,
lying on the ground,
the smell of the earth,
song of a bird,
a fleeting cloud.
This is my real home,
my spiritual sense of being breathes slowly,
    deeply.
My architecture is for when it rains,
when the wind blows,
when darkness invades my heart,
when I have been on the move
and am not allowed to rest with my shadow.
If I have the sun and if the night is warm, I am
    content in the grass.
To find my shadow,
my delight in my architecture,
my home,

is to allow my soul to meet my momentarily still
    fleeting self.
This is my home,
my sanctuary in a hurry-hurry noisy-noisy
    rough-tough world.
This is where my shadow and I shelter,
inhabit, with my habits.
Perhaps my habits are the expressions of me,
my freedom to repeat them,
to know them,
to live with them an essential part of my being
    and my identity.
Perhaps I inhabit my habits rather than my
    architecture,
or the grass slope of a hill under the sun.
Perhaps my habits are simply me building
    memories –
a digital camera in my pocket,
a sketchbook open –
writing these words,
a conversation over a nice meal and a delicate
    wine.

Who will remember my habits?
keep my memories –
surely not the walls or spaces of my house?
The future can only recall that I 'lived' here – a
    name plaque on a wall.
So it is a habit and memory,
encounter, love, laughter and tears
that forever holds the spirit of place –
is this why there are so many ghosts in theatres?
When we leave home, we have e_migrated,
and we are changed forever when we migrate.
We have decided to leave,
we have left, and even if we do return
it is to the place we left,
not the home we knew,
not home any more.
This is the century
where city urbanites outnumber the agrarians
for the first time in human history.
Present agrarians have not migrated,
they know their soil, their home.
Every modern nomad knows this.

He also knows that the whole world is his home
even if he cannot physically travel there.
The nomad is not bound, or blinkered by
    owning his bricks and mortar!
He belongs to one Earth (a global society)
far more than the jet-travelling businessman.

'How easy it is to lose sight of what is historically invisible
– as if people lived only history and nothing else.'
    John Berger

ON THE RIM OF REASON: THE PULSE FROM EDGE TO THE CENTRE AND OUT AGAIN

I came to architecture from the edge,
somewhere between the edge of medicine and the
   edge of art,
wanting to help people and to express myself.
Both my humanity and my art were intuitive.
I think I was lucky with my DNA
and the access I had to nature's wonders.
I lived on the edge of architecture
yet the actions were central.
I thought, I drew, and I built,
but I thought about society as much as form.
I drew with a Rapidograph but also with a brush.
I tried investigating free-time space,
and speculating on where urbanism was going.
I realised architecture in East Anglia,
and saw egos and business competitiveness.
I built real buildings with my own hands,
then taught architecture, but not really.
I had insufficient knowledge, but
I nurtured the students and
shared building buildings with them.
Then I began to explore engineering,
while exploring a partnership,
and working and learning at Arup.
I worked with industry, I researched,
and I dirtied my hands in the workshop.
And the boundaries of architecture
that had begun to appear began to dissolve
and I saw that I was out on the edge.
I began an open partnership in France,
no boundaries other than the sensual
nature of buildings and streets, and
materials, light, landscape and technique.
I remained on the edge but in the centre
of French political ambition.
Seminal exposés of public performance
and technical innovation.
A knowledge and feel for glass
that brought me to the centre,
because the image was potent
and sought after throughout Europe,
and later in the US. But I had cracked
glass, and wanted to move outward again,
to weave and deploy new materials
that would evoke new ideas and spaces.
I had knowledge, I became an 'uncle',
maybe even wise, as I began giving back to society.
I am moving to the edge again, happy.
And now I write as much as I draw.
My imagination is still on the rim of reason
and I do not know my next architecture,
but my responsibility is still towards humanity
and my memories give me strength
for future work, play and life I share.